TV AND VIDEO

INGRID GESER

MEDIA STORY

MEDIA STORY

ADVERTISING

BOOKS

COMICS AND MAGAZINES

FILMS

PLAYS

TV AND VIDEO

Series Designer: Helen White
Editor: Janet De Saulles

Cover: Videos of feature films and television programmes can be
bought or rented.

First published in 1990 by
Wayland (Publishers) Ltd
61 Western Road, Hove
East Sussex BN3 1JD

Phototypeset by Direct Image Photosetting Ltd., Hove, Sussex,
England
Printed in Italy by G. Canale & C.S.p.A.
Bound in Portsmouth by MacLehose

British Library Cataloguing in Publication Data
Geser, Ingrid
Television and Video.
1. Television programmes. Production
I. Title   II. Series
791.450232
ISBN 1-85210-916-5

CONTENTS

THE USES OF TV AND VIDEO

TELEVISION AND video are two of the most popular and exciting forms of modern entertainment. Every day millions of people all over the world switch on a television set or a video cassette recorder (VCR). In this book you will see how television programmes and videos are made, and you will be shown how to make a programme yourself.

Music videos are an increasingly popular form of entertainment, receiving a sizeable amount of television airtime.

**The television comedy
'A Different World' was made and
first broadcast in the USA.**

Why do we watch television programmes and videos? There are three main reasons: they entertain, they inform and they educate. Comedies entertain us by making us laugh, while news programmes inform by telling us what is happening all over the world. Television programmes and videos can also educate: a programme about the American Civil War, for example, can create a strong impression of what it was like to live in that period.

A VCR can be used to record television programmes so they can be watched at any time. You can also buy or hire films and other programmes on video, or even make your own programmes using a video camera.

Each television company has at least one channel on which its programmes are shown or **transmitted**. Some channels specialize in a particular kind of programme, for example MTV in the USA screens non-stop music. Television companies are always battling amongst themselves. This is known as the **ratings** war. The programme watched by the most people goes to the top of the ratings.

There are many types of television programme. Over the page are some of the types you might have seen:

**Video rental shops can be found
in many parts of the world.**

5

- Educational programmes – these help you to learn; an example is a schools science programme.
- Documentaries – factual programmes; an example might be a programme on cruelty to animals.
- Current affairs programmes – these deal with topics that are in the news.
- Light entertainment – these are light-hearted programmes, such as quiz shows and comedies.
- Soap operas – dramas that deal with everyday life.
- Natural history – programmes about wildlife and nature.

This photograph shows Jason Donovan as seen on the MTV Sky television channel.

Videos deal with some of these subjects too, and they can be specially useful for teaching. They can be used to show people how to do a particular job, such as how to be a good telephone receptionist. Some big companies like to show videos of how they work to new employees or customers. These are called corporate videos.

An incredible amount of work goes into making any television programme or video. This book looks at some of the efforts that go on behind the scenes in turning an idea into a programme or video that will be watched by millions of viewers.

RIGHT **Justine Clarke and Alex Papps have leading roles in 'Home and Away'.**

BELOW **Anglia television's natural history programmes are popular with viewers.**

RESEARCHING A PROGRAMME

The idea

THE FIRST stage in making a video or television programme is having the idea. This might come from watching other programmes, from reading about something interesting, or from being concerned about something that is going on in the world.

BBC researchers finding out information for the current affairs programme 'Question Time'.

Sam and Emma – two of the characters in the Australian soap 'The Flying Doctors'.

Programme devisers, people whose job it is to have ideas for television programmes, usually write down their ideas as they have them. Many keep a notebook by their bed, as ideas often spring to mind at night. Ideas have to be turned into pictures, so these will be jotted down alongside the ideas.

Unless you are making a programme for only yourself or friends to see, the next step is to persuade a **television production company** that your idea is worth developing, and that people will want to watch the end result. To do this, you need to have a clear idea of what you want to say in the programme (the message), at whom the programme is aimed (the audience), and how you want to present it (the treatment).

To be sure of what you want to do, you need to **research** your idea thoroughly. First of all, find out as much as you can about the topic in which you are interested. Go to your local library and read whatever you can find on the subject in books, magazines and newspapers. The librarian will help you find information. You could also contact any organizations that have a special interest in the topic. They may have information packs, or their own videos that you could watch.

While you are researching, keep a note of any information you might want to use in the programme, including people you might want to interview and possible places you might want to use for filming.

Channel Four's 'Survivor's Guide' appeals to teenagers' interests.

**Feature films such as 'Who Framed Roger Rabbit?'
are made for the cinema but are released on
video soon afterwards.**

ABOVE Quiz shows are popular with audiences because of the incredible prizes that can be won.

BELOW National and local news programmes are shown daily at regular intervals.

The audience

The most important consideration for any programme maker is the audience. Television programming is organized very carefully with each channel having its programmes shown at an appropriate time of the day or evening. These different times are called slots and are aimed at certain groups of people. For example, the 5.15 to 5.45 pm slot might be aimed at teenagers, because this is a time when they are likely to be home from school.

To understand how programming is arranged, look at the television programmes listed on two competing channels on the same weekday.

● Write down the group of people at which you think each programme is aimed.

- Is there a particular time of day when there are programmes for people your age?
- Do both channels show programmes for the same group of people at the same time?
- If you were a programme controller, in which slot would you place the following types of programme: a soap opera (such as *EastEnders,* or *Neighbours)*, a natural history programme, a cartoon?

Presentation

Once you have decided on your idea and audience, you need to work out your presentation or treatment. This is the general **style** of the programme.

Your first consideration should be the audience. Its age will influence the way in which you present your video or programme. If you were making a video for four-to seven-year-olds on how to look after teeth you would present it in a different way from a programme on

An outdoor set at Universal City Studios in the USA. Special screens ensure the light is spread evenly over the set.

The studo lighting and background give a sober, historical feel to this programme.

the same topic for eight- to eleven-year-olds. A typical approach for the younger age group would be to use popular cartoon figures as the main characters, and perhaps a superhero figure like Batman for the older children. A teenage audience might prefer a pop star. The message would be the same for all age groups – look after your teeth or they will rot – but the presentation would be different.

The type of programme or video you are making will also affect your presentation. News programmes are serious, whereas game shows are light-hearted. The mood of the programme is reflected in the **set**, with perhaps a desk and plain backdrop for a news programme, but bright colours and special effects for a quiz show.

Each type of programme uses a standard **format**. An interview usually starts with a shot of the interviewer, followed by a shot of the guest. There may then be shots of both of them together, or of whoever is talking.

The topic you choose and the way you want to present it will help you decide whether to film in a television studio or **on location**. News programmes are a mixture of studio filming, where the presenter reads the

News programmes are normally made up of a mixture of on location shots and studio shots.

headlines, and of special reports filmed outside the studio. These are known as **outside broadcasts**.

If you have an idea for a programme, you can either write to the producer of a similar programme (this will appear in the **credits** at the end), or you can write to independent television production companies. Your local library may have a list of these. Look for a company that has made programmes on similar topics and send them a typed summary of your ideas. This should list:

● What the programme or video will be about.

The studio set for the BBC chat show 'Wogan' is simple and uncluttered.

● Why you want to make it.
● How long it will last. This should be no longer than 30 minutes.
● The audience you are aiming at.
● The way you think the information should be presented.

Experienced programme devisers usually include an estimate of how many days filming are required, and an estimate of how much the programme will cost to make.

PRODUCING A PROGRAMME

IF YOU are lucky enough to have your idea accepted then the whole process of **production** will now get under way. There may be hundreds of people involved in turning an idea into a programme or video, or there may be only a handful, depending on the size of the production.

The television dramatization of one of C. S. Lewis's popular 'Narnia' books was enjoyed by both children and adults.

The producer is usually involved in a programme or video from the beginning. It is the producer's job to estimate how much it will cost to make the programme, to raise the money, and then to keep within this budget. Filming is extremely expensive. Some of the expenses a producer might have to take into consideration are costumes, film crew, equipment hire, scenery, transport, special effects and catering.

If the producer does not have time to research a programme, he or she employs somebody, or a team of people, to do part of the work. Detailed research involves reading about the

ABOVE The budget for 'Crocodile Dundee' had to cover expenses for special effects and the film crew.

OPPOSITE Films such as this can be rented on video. For any feature film, detailed research must take place.

topic, watching other programmes and videos on the same subject, and possibly arranging for short pieces or clips from these to be used. The researcher also looks for people to be interviewed and goes on '**recces**' to check possible sites for filming.

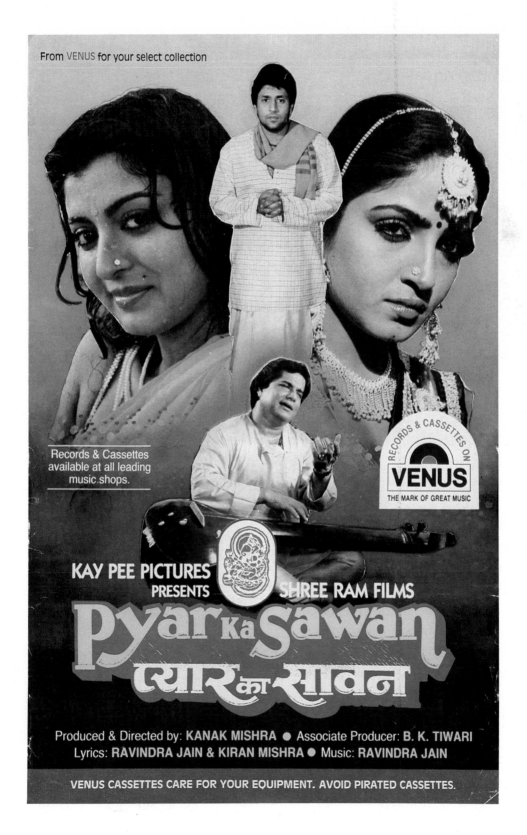

Ed Bradley is the television presenter for the US news programme '60 Minutes'.

Once the research has been done, it is time for the producer to plan the programme in detail. This may include writing a **script**. Although television can bring ideas powerfully to life, it is not always good at putting over too many facts at once. It is normally advisable to keep to five or six main points in a factual programme.

When planning the programme, the producer has to keep in mind how each point will look on film, and make sure that the programme will hold the audience's attention. Long periods of talking, in soap operas for example, can be boring to watch and are usually broken up by 'business', such as actors washing up, walking about, making a drink and so on. This activity is not part of the story but is more interesting to watch than two people simply sitting still and talking.

Producers are responsible for managing the presenters involved in a programme or video. Whether they work on a serious news programme or a light-hearted quiz show, it is the presenter's job to present the programme in a clear way and to keep calm, no matter what happens. Presenters look as if they are just chatting to the camera, but in fact they usually have to read from a roller prompter, such as an autocue. This displays about eight lines of type, 15mm high, which roll past as the presenter reads them. Newsreaders have a copy of the script on their desks. They also have an **ear-piece** link with the director, so that they can hear any instructions.

Newsreaders read their stories out from a roller prompter.

FILMING

FILMING INVOLVES an enormous amount of planning. Everyone has to know what is expected of them before work starts. In this section of the book you will see what sort of organization and planning go on before filming begins in a television studio.

The complicated 'Dragnet' set for MCA—TV in Hollywood required detailed organization.

The studio

Television centres usually have several studios of varying sizes. The major part of the studio floor is taken up by the setting area, where the scenery goes. Lights are hung or clamped to a framework on the ceiling or on to special stands. On the walls are power supplies, lighting controls, scenery hoists and sockets.

It is the director's job to turn the script into a finished programme or video. The director tells the other people involved in the filming what the programme is about and what style it will be presented in. They then get to work on

This man is testing transmission signals in preparation for a television broadcast.

their individual tasks. For example, the **set designer** may make a card model of the set to check that the cameras will be able to move about the set easily, and the lighting director will work to create the right sort of mood with the lighting. The director rehearses the actors or presenters, and decides where the cameras should be situated. The technical director organizes any special effects and the sound engineers check microphone links.

A film crew in Pakistan working on the programme 'Afghan Women'.

Before filming begins, most directors prepare a 'shooting script'. This is a plan of the filming. It shows who and what is being filmed, when this will take place and in what order. Some programmes are shown or screened live. This means that what you see on your screen is actually happening at that moment in the studio. If any mistakes are made, you see them as they happen. The news is an example of a live programme. However, most programmes are recorded and then shown later.

In a studio production, the cameras are placed around the actors, presenters or guests (known as talent). There are between two and five cameras and these are usually wheeled around on mobile supports. The camera operators have to make sure that the picture is in focus, that it is well composed (for example, the person's head is not cut off), and that they have the kind of shot the director has asked for. The camera operators wear headphones, or 'cans', so that they can hear instructions from the director in the control room.

A floor manager, who also wears headphones, looks after any studio guests and passes on instructions from the director. Preparations for filming take a long time. Lighting has to be adjusted, make-up retouched, and sound checked. The floor manager

The Australian film 'Young Einstein' starred Yahoo Serious.

This studio shot of news presenter Moira Stewart has been filmed in close-up.

explains to guests what is going on, and where they should stand, marking this with tape. When recording is about to start, the floor manager uses special hand signals to warn everyone. Then a red light comes on outside the studio, so that no one comes into or leaves the studio.

The gallery

Pictures from the cameras and sound from the studio microphones pass to a control room, or gallery, where quality is checked and any special effects, such as music are added. The director sits at a control desk with the vision mixer. The director tells the vision mixer which camera's shot should be recorded or transmitted, and the vision mixer presses the appropriate controls. The director's assistant and the technical

director also sit in the control room. In front of them are a series of **monitors**, displaying what each camera is focused on. The director uses shorthand terms to describe which shots the camera operators should get. A CU is a close-up shot, showing the person's head and shoulders, and a LS is a long shot, showing the whole body. When a camera's shot is being recorded, a red light on top of the camera comes on, so that the presenters and actors know which camera they should be facing.

The director's assistant calls out the shots, announcing which shot is being recorded from which camera, and which shot is next. 'Shot 27 on 4, 2 next', means that shot 27 is being recorded from camera four, and camera two's shot will be recorded next.

At the end of a recording, the director

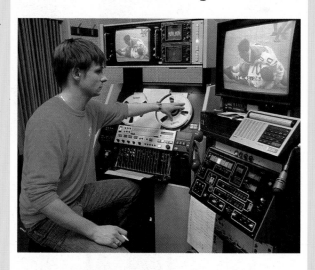

Images from a number of cameras are passed through to the control room.

runs through the tape to make sure that everything is alright. If not, some scenes may need to be reshot.

Outside broadcasts

Outside broadcasts are programmes, or parts of programmes, filmed outside the television studio (although not necessarily outdoors). A mobile control room is used to record the pictures and transmit them to the television station. Outside broadcasts usually require special arrangements, such as

BELOW 'Upstairs Downstairs' was filmed at the London Weekend Television Studios.

ABOVE Senator Edward Kennedy being video-taped during a speech.

permission for filming. The weather, power supplies, transport, and accommodation for the film crew also need to be taken into consideration. So that the cameras can run along smoothly, special track may have to be laid down. Other special equipment might include camera filters that create a night-time effect. Filming at night is awkward and expensive, so directors save time and money by filming during the day with this filter. You can often tell that one has been used by the presence of puffy white clouds through the darkness.

Recording sound on location can be extremely difficult. The sound recordist has to make sure that no background noises, such as the sound of a passing aeroplane, are also recorded. This is particularly important in historical

Storyboards show positions of people and objects.

programmes. The sound of an aircraft flying by in an educational video on nineteenth-century Australia would totally destroy the atmosphere and the programme's credibility.

Unless the programme is going out live, filming is not necessarily done in the same sequence as it will be shown. Instead, it is organized into groups of shots so that, for example, all the scenes in the same location are filmed at the same time. The film is later edited into the right order. In some productions, drawings showing the positions of people and objects are used. These are called storyboards and they show the exact shots the director wants.

EDITING

UNLESS A programme is recorded **live-on-tape**, a lot of work still has to be done before the programme or video is ready for transmission. In the **editing suite**, the director and editor go through all the recorded material and decide which shots to use. Like film, video tape records a series of still **frames**, which appear to move at normal speed when they are run at twenty-five frames per second.

These editors are going through each film, deciding which are the best shots to use.

Many illusions can be created: a shot of a snake might be set next to one of an actor to give the impression of close combat.

First of all, a digital clock read-out is recorded on to the videotape, so that each frame has a time code noted against it. The director can note the time code of each shot required, so that the editor knows which shots to edit together.

Editing can create some wonderful illusions. Have you ever watched a television programme in which a man meets a lion but manages to run away from it? Were you amazed that the lion did not attack him? In fact, the two probably never even met. They were filmed against similar backgrounds at different times. The shots were then edited to create the impression that the person and the animal were there together. Sometimes it is obvious that filming has been done on separate occasions. Look at the sky and background in each shot to see if they are the same. Often you will find that the sky is a slightly different colour, or cloudier in one shot.

The editor has to make sure that all cuts between shots are smooth. You may have noticed on television or video that the picture sometimes appears to jump. This is usually due to bad editing.

Sometimes an editor will find that, at a vital point in the tape, someone walks in front of the camera, ruining the shot. Camera crews normally take a number of shots that can be edited over these problem areas. They include reaction shots, for example a crowd's reaction to a speech, and 'noddies', shots of the interviewer nodding with interest.

You will remember that, during filming, a lot of care was put into sound recording, and making sure that there were no unwanted background noises. Despite this, sound is often **dubbed** once the tape has been edited. The sound engineer and director want as much control over the sound-track as possible. Let's say a certain scene requires the sound of rain. Even if the crew were lucky enough to shoot the scene on a wet day, the sound of the rain might well have been too quiet or may even have been mixed with other noises, such as passing traffic. The sound engineer might have to use a library tape of the sound of rain to dub over the sound-track.

Commentary is often added in the editing suite too. This has to be written to the right length and spoken at the right speed (about three words per second) so that it coincides with the pictures. The editor also adds the programme titles and the credits.

Once the edited version of the tape is ready, the director watches it all the way through to check that everything is alright.

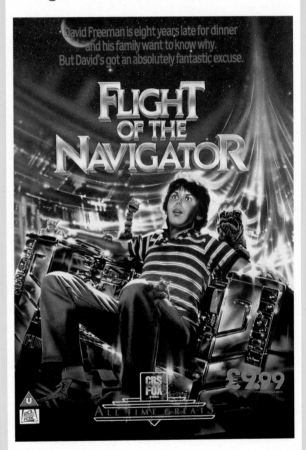

The editor of 'Flight of the Navigator' had to make sure that the sound-track coincided exactly with the images on film.

MAKING YOUR OWN VIDEO

ONE WAY to experience the excitement and problems of making a programme is to make your own video. You can do this on your own or as part of a group.

Pictures from magazines can be used as stills for your video.

Video cameras are easy to operate. You may be able to borrow one from a relative or a local video production group, or you can hire one from a shop. If you cannot get a camera, you can still plan a video to get an idea of how much work is involved.

Before you get the camera, spend some time planning your project. You might want to make a documentary about something like pollution, or a programme about your favourite sport, hobby or pop group. When you have researched the topic, pick five or six points that you want to make and decide how you will illustrate them. You might want to film somebody talking about the subject and use **stills** from newspapers and magazines as illustrations. Next, prepare a storyboard. Draw a rough picture of each shot you want to film, including the title and credits (these can be written on card). Under each picture, write the script that will accompany it and make a note of any music or sound effects.

Unless you can get somebody to edit the tape for you, you will have to shoot live-on-tape, so the finished video will be just as you shoot it. (Although you can record over any mistakes you make.) For this reason it is a good idea to have a full rehearsal before you start filming. Play back each scene as soon as you have recorded it (the camera should have a tiny monitor for this), so that you can reshoot if necessary.

Try to keep the programme active by getting the people in it to move around, or by filming something lively, like a local pop group. You may need some practice before you can film people walking; the best way is to shoot them from a diagonal angle. Make sure you

Once you have decided on your ideas you can begin filming.

leave a little space above their heads in each frame.

Do not make your programme too long, or your viewers will get bored. Aim for around ten minutes for your first video. You will be surprised at how much work goes into such a short programme. When you have made your video, all that there remains to do is to watch it. Perhaps seeing it will give you ideas for making some more!

GLOSSARY

Commentary A description of what is going on.

Credits A list of people who helped make a programme, video or film.

Dubbed When another sound-track is added to a programme.

Ear-piece A listening device, worn in the ear.

Editing suite The rooms in which videotape or film is cut and rearranged into the right order.

Format Style or arrangement.

Frames Individual exposures on a film.

Live-on-tape Video recorded without cuts or editing.

Monitors Television sets.

On location When something is filmed or recorded where the action takes place, outside the studio.

Outside broadcasts (OBs) Programmes, or parts of programmes, that are shot outside the studio (although not necessarily outdoors).

Production The making, and preparation for making, a television programme or video.

Ratings These measure the size of an audience for a particular television programme.

Recces Visits to possible sites for filming.

Research To search carefully for information.

Script The words of a video or television programme.

Set The background or scenery of a show.

Set designer Someone who designs the scenery for a television programme or video.

Stills Pictures that do not move, such as photographs and slides.

Style The way in which a programme is presented or treated.

Television production companies Companies that make programmes for televison.

Transmitted When television programmes are sent out over the air so that viewers can watch them.

BOOKS TO READ

Doctor Who: The Making of a Television Series by Alan Road (André Deutsch, 1982)
Inside Story: Television by Tim Byrne and Tony Gregory (Wayland, 1989)
Television by Keith Wicks (Granada, 1983)
Television and Video by Manuel Alvarado (Wayland, 1987)
TV and Video by N. S. Barrett (Franklin Watts, 1985)

ACKNOWLEDGEMENTS

The Publisher would like to thank the following for providing the pictures used in this book: Aquarius 6, 11 (top), 12, 13 (top), 18 (bottom), 19, 24; BBC Enterprises 22 (top); Channel Four 5 (top), 9 (bottom); Format 21 (top); Kobal 10, 16, 21 (bottom), 23 (bottom); Photri 11 (bottom), 13 (bottom), 18 (top), 23 (top), 25; Rex 7 (top), 9 (top), 29; Paul Seheult COVER, 4, 17, 27, 28; Survival Anglia 7 (bottom), 26; Topham 8, 14, 15, 20, 22 (bottom); Wayland Picture Library 5 (bottom).

INDEX

The numbers in **bold** refer to captions